When Time Began

Copyright © 1993 by Hunt & Thorpe

Published in Nashville, Tennessee, by Oliver-Nelson Books, a
division of Thomas Nelson, Inc., Publishers, and distributed in
Canada by Lawson Falle, Ltd., Cambridge, Ontario.

Printed in Malaysia

Library of Congress Cataloging-in-Publication Data

Pipe, Rhona.
When time began/Rhona Pipe; illustrated by Jenny Press.
p. cm. — (Now I can read Bible stories)
Summary: A simple retelling of the Bible story in which God
created the world in six days.
ISBN 0-8407-3419-0
1. Creation — Biblical teaching — Juvenile literature. 2. Bible
stories, English — O.T. Genesis. (1. Creation. 2. Bible stories —
O.T.) I. Press. Jenny, ill. II. Title. III. Series.
BS651-P544. 1992
222′.1109505 — dc20

92-13321
CIP
AC

1 2 3 4 5 6 — 98 97 96 95 94 93

When Time Began

Rhona Pipe

Illustrated by
Jenny Press

OLIVER
NELSON

THOMAS NELSON PUBLISHERS
Nashville

When time began,
God made the earth.
It had no life.
It had no shape.
It was boiling and black.
And God's Spirit moved
over the earth.

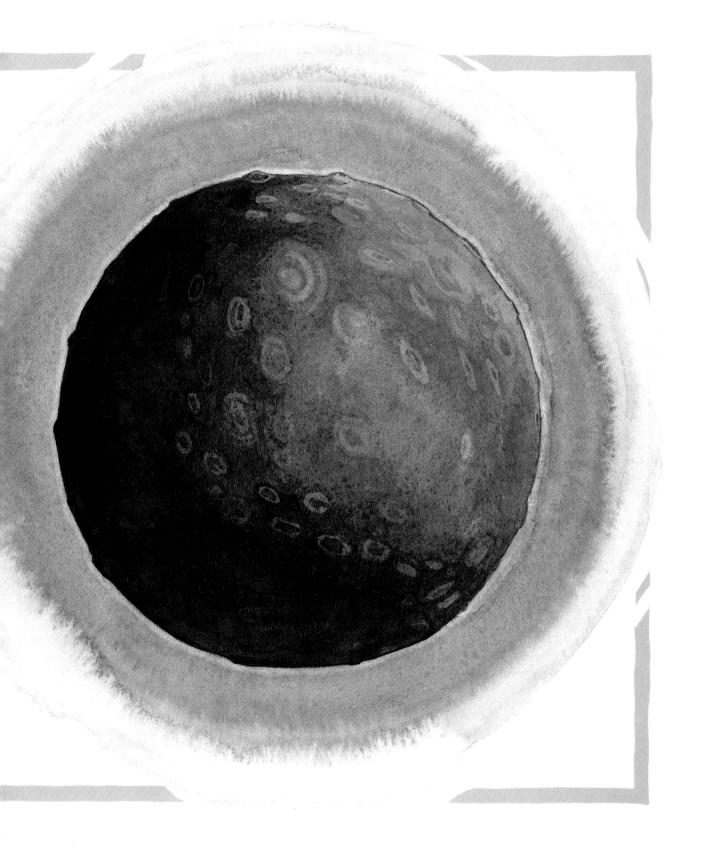

God said,
"Let there be light."
And light came.
God was glad
when He saw the light.
He named the light *day*.
And He named
the darkness *night*.
That was Day One in the
making of the earth.

Then God said,

"Let there be a roof over the earth.

Let it keep some waters
above the earth.

Let it keep some waters
on the earth."

And it was done.

God named the roof *sky*.

That was Day Two in the making
of the earth.

Then God said,
"Let the waters come together.
Let there be dry land."
And it was done.
God named the waters *seas*
and the land *earth*.
God was glad when He saw
the seas and the earth.

Then God said,
"Let plants with seeds grow
on the earth.
Let trees with fruit grow
on the earth."
And it was done.
God was glad when He saw the
plants and trees.
That was Day Three in the
making of the earth.

Then God said,
"Let lights come in the sky.
Let the lights shine down
on the earth."
And it was done.
God made the sun for the day.
God made the moon and stars
for the night.
He was glad
when He saw the lights.
That was Day Four in the
making of the earth.

Then God said,
"Let fish fill the seas.
Let birds fly in the sky."
And it was done.
God was glad when He saw the fish.
God was glad when He saw the birds.
He said, "Be happy
and grow in number."
That was Day Five in the
making of the earth.

Then God said,
"Let animals live on the earth.
Let the animals be big and small."
And it was done.
And God was glad when He saw
the animals.

Last of all God said,
"Now We will make people.
We will make men and
women like Us.
They will look after the fish
and the birds.
They will look after the animals
on the earth." And it was done.
And God said, "Be happy and
grow in number. You have
grain and fruit to eat."

God looked at what He had made.

It was very good.

He was glad.

That was the end of Day Six.

It was the end of making the earth.

God did not work on Day Seven.

He said, "Day Seven is a happy day.

It is a day to rest.

It is a day to praise Me."